A CIGAR LOVER'S JOURNAL

A Journal of Cigars & Special Times Enjoyed by

A CIGAR LOVER'S JOURNAL

With an introduction
by
André Saint-Jacques

RAINCOAST BOOKS

Vancouver

First published in 1999 by

Raincoast Books
8680 Cambie Street
Vancouver, B.C.
V6P 6M9
(604) 323-7100
www.raincoast.com

1 2 3 4 5 6 7 8 9 10

CANADIAN CATALOGUING IN PUBLICATION DATA

Main entry under title:
A cigar lover's journal
ISBN 1-55192-268-1
1. Cigars – Miscellanea. 2. Diaries (Blank-books)
TS2260.C55 1999   679'.72   C99-910390-3

Raincoast Books gratefully acknowledges the support of the Government of Canada, through the Book Publishing Industry Development Program, the Canada Council for the Arts and the Department of Canadian Heritage. We also acknowledge the assistance of the Province of British Columbia, through the British Columbia Arts Council.

Cover Photograph by Joseph Marranca
Illustrations by Thomas Anfield
Printed and bound in Canada

Contents

Cigar Tasting: From First Light to Last Draw
by André Saint-Jacques
2

Cigar-Tasting Notes & Experiences
7

Cigars to Try Next Time
98

Addresses & Contact Numbers
104

Cigar Labels & Miscellanea
110

Cigar-Smoking Terms
117

Cigar Tasting:
From First Light to Last Draw

My earliest "cigar" smoking memories take me back to the age of 10, when I used to sneak down to the edge of the dock to enjoy a wine-tipped Colt. Back then, I thought I was pretty cool. Who would have thought that, years later, cigars would become my life, and that I would be selling them all over North America?

The cigar's rich and colorful history dates back to October 28, 1492, when Christopher Columbus first arrived on the island of Cuba. There, he and fellow explorer, Rodriguo de Xeres, found both the male and female Natives puffing away on "little lighted brands." De Xeres, first to join the Natives in a smoke, is considered the original Western discoverer of the cigar. According to historians, it wasn't until the mid-eighteenth century that the cigar made its first appearance in North America. Today, approximately 600 million cigars are smoked on this continent each year.

Just as wine grapes are affected by variations in soil and climate, so too are tobacco plants. Such variations can produce anything from subtle to striking differences in the taste of the final product. A cigar's flavor very much depends on where the tobacco was grown, what factory it was harvested from and how long it has been aged.

It takes anywhere from three to four months for a tobacco seed to develop into a full-grown plant that is ready for harvest. Once fully developed, the plant leaves are cut and hung in barns

> *A cigar ought not to be smoked solely with the mouth, but with the hand, the eyes and with the spirit.*
>
> ——— ≭◊≊ ———
>
> Zino Davidoff

for approximately 45 to 60 days. During this time, the color of the leaves will ideally change from a dark green to a golden brown. The leaves are then piled into "bulks" and dampened in order to promote the initial stage of fermentation, a delicate process that lasts up to three months and removes the impurities from the tobacco. They are then sorted into three categories — wrapper, filler and binder — and the second stage of fermentation, which can take between one and two months, begins. Once fermentation is complete, the leaves are stored in a factory or a warehouse, where they will mature further for anywhere from 16 to 24 months. When the aging process is complete, the tobacco is ready for the rolling stage. Without a doubt, handmade (as opposed to machine-made) cigars are of the best quality.

Evaluating a cigar is similar to evaluating a glass of wine. Like fine wines, cigars are described by their appearance and flavor. To begin making notes on a cigar, first assess how it looks. Start by looking at the wrapper. It should be perfect: no wrinkles, spots, veins or tears. Your cigar should also be moist. This may not be obvious to the eye, so take the cigar between your thumb and forefinger and press on it gently. A cigar that has been properly hand-rolled and humidified will be firm but resilient; in other words, it will spring back without the sound of cracking tobacco. After lighting your cigar, have a look at the ash. Color and structure are important. The whiter the ash, the better the soil in which the tobacco was grown, and a long, evenly formed ash is a sign of a well-constructed cigar.

Cigars can deliver a wide variety of tastes. To evaluate the flavor of a cigar, hold the smoke in your mouth for a few seconds (*never* inhale it into your lungs) and allow your tongue and upper palate to savor the different taste sensations. A cigar's flavors can range from sweet (with hints of cinnamon, vanilla or cocoa) to spicy (with characteristics of pepper, nutmeg and other robust herbs) to woody (with suggestions of cedar or oak). The range of flavors goes on and on, from acidic, bitter and salty to rich, heavy and full-bodied.

Another thing to observe when evaluating a cigar is its draw (the rate at which air is pulled through a lit cigar). If it draws quickly and fills your mouth with hot rather than cool, tasty smoke, it is a poorly made cigar, often referred to as "hot." Similarly, if the cigar is hard to draw on, or if it goes out two or three times before you've smoked a third of it, it has likely been wrapped too tightly. Such a cigar is often referred to as "plugged." A cigar's draw should be smooth and easy. Depending on the size, you should get about 50 puffs from a well-made cigar, and it should burn anywhere from 30 minutes to one and a half hours.

Cigar shapes and sizes vary from brand to brand, so it is important to note the length and diameter of your cigar. Length is recorded in either inches or centimeters, and diameter (known as "ring gauge") is measured in 1/64ths of an inch (or 0.4 millimeters). Therefore, a cigar with a ring gauge of 32 is 32/64ths of an inch (or 12.5 millimeters) in diameter. Remember that, in general, cigars with large ring gauges tend to have more flavor than those that are smaller in diameter. The reason is quite simple: thicker cigars are often made with three or four different kinds of tobacco, while cigars with smaller ring gauges normally hold only two (or at most three) types of tobacco.

If you are new to cigar smoking, I recommend that you begin with a mild blend and then work your way up to a more full-bodied cigar. This will allow your taste buds to adjust gradually to the many flavors of the cigars available. Start by choosing a light-bodied cigar with a sweet taste, one from Jamaica or the Dominican Republic, for example. When you are ready for a more robust smoke, try a Cuban cigar (an experience to be truly savored). In the end, there are no hard and fast rules regarding what you should or shouldn't smoke. The cigar that you enjoy is the right one for you.

Finally, a few points of etiquette. Never light a cigar with a candle or a regular match. The candle wax or the sulfur from the match can add an unpleasant flavor to your cigar. Aficionados use cedar matches or a butane lighter. Never crush a cigar on completion. It should die a slow, smoldering death (one that will release less odor than if you stamp it out). I prefer to remove the cigar band before beginning to smoke. After all, a cigar is highly attractive in its nudity, and the band makes a great keepsake. However, it is not considered *déclassé* to smoke your cigar with the band on. Smoke in a well-ventilated room and avoid smoking in the presence of food. Finally, remember to smoke slowly. If you take more than two puffs a minute, your cigar may overheat, which will ruin its taste.

A Cigars Lover's Journal is a unique record book in which you can not only chronicle the details of each cigar you've smoked but also document the occasions in which the cigars were enjoyed. Looking back through my journals, I realize that many of my smoking experiences are linked to some of the most memorable times of my life: enjoying a cigar over a vintage Scotch and great conversation, lighting a cigar during an intense round of golf or passing out cigars at the close of a successful business deal. My cigar journals are a walk down memory lane.

One becomes a cigar connoisseur with experience. So, experiment with the wide variety of cigars available, and remember to pay attention to each cigar's unique characteristics. This classic journal is designed to help you chronicle some of the information that you will absorb, so, at a minimum, I encourage you to write down the brand name, the country, the length and ring gauge and the cost and purchase date of each cigar that you light. Take *A Cigar Lover's Journal* with you each and every time you are about to savor the moment by lighting a cigar. The longer the cigar, the more time you will have for reflection.

Finally, sit back, relax and enjoy! As George Sand once said, "The cigar is the perfect complement to an elegant lifestyle."

André Saint-Jacques

> *The most futile and*
> *disastrous day seems*
> *well spent when it is*
> *reviewed through the*
> *blue, fragrant smoke*
> *of a Havana cigar.*

Evelyn Waugh

Cigar-Tasting Notes
& Experiences

Cigar Notes

Brand
Region/Country
Vintage
Length
Ring Gauge
Date Purchased
Place of Purchase
Price/Quantity

Rating

Exceptional		*Smokable*	
Most Enjoyable		*Poor*	

Affix Cigar Band Here

Tasting Notes

Appearance/Ash
Burn/Draw
Flavor/Strength
Overall Impressions

Tasting Experience

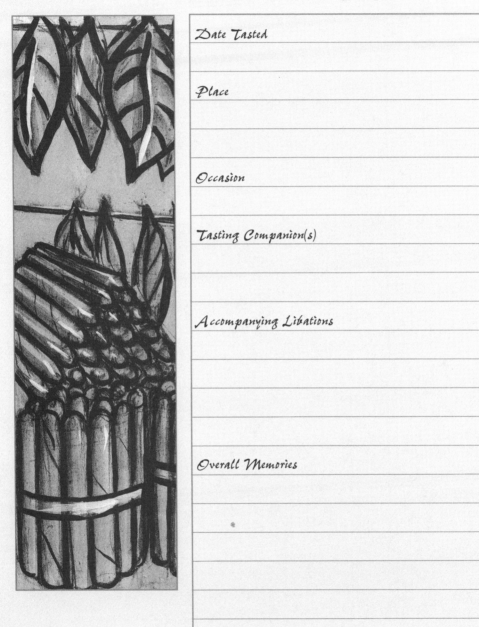

Date Tasted

Place

Occasion

Tasting Companion(s)

Accompanying Libations

Overall Memories

Cigar Notes

Brand
Region/Country
Vintage
Length
Ring Gauge
Date Purchased
Place of Purchase
Price/Quantity

Rating

Exceptional		Smokable	
Most Enjoyable		Poor	

Affix Cigar Band Here

Tasting Notes

Appearance/Ash
Burn/Draw
Flavor/Strength
Overall Impressions

Tasting Experience

Date Tasted

Place

Occasion

Tasting Companion(s)

Accompanying Libations

Overall Memories

Cigar Notes

Brand
Region/Country
Vintage
Length
Ring Gauge
Date Purchased
Place of Purchase
Price/Quantity

Rating

Exceptional

Smokable

Most Enjoyable

Poor

Affix Cigar Band Here

Tasting Notes

Appearance/Ash
Burn/Draw
Flavor/Strength
Overall Impressions

Tasting Experience

> I haven't been sick a
> day since I was a
> child. A steady diet
> of cigars and
> whiskey cured me.
>
> ————❖————
>
> W. C. Fields

Date Tasted

Place

Occasion

Tasting Companion(s)

Accompanying Libations

Overall Memories

Cigar Notes

Brand
Region/Country
Vintage
Length
Ring Gauge
Date Purchased
Place of Purchase
Price/Quantity

Rating

Exceptional		Smokable	
Most Enjoyable		Poor	

Affix Cigar Band Here

Tasting Notes

Appearance/Ash
Burn/Draw
Flavor/Strength
Overall Impressions

Tasting Experience

Date Tasted

Place

Occasion

Tasting Companion(s)

Accompanying Libations

Overall Memories

Cigar Notes

Brand	
Region/Country	
Vintage	
Length	
Ring Gauge	
Date Purchased	
Place of Purchase	
Price/Quantity	

Rating

Exceptional		Smokable	
Most Enjoyable		Poor	

Affix Cigar Band Here

Tasting Notes

Appearance/Ash
Burn/Draw
Flavor/Strength
Overall Impressions

Tasting Experience

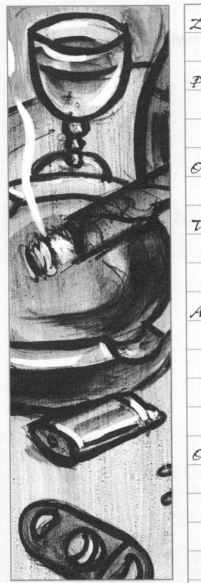

Date Tasted

Place

Occasion

Tasting Companion(s)

Accompanying Libations

Overall Memories

Cigar Notes

Brand
Region/Country
Vintage
Length
Ring Gauge
Date Purchased
Place of Purchase
Price/Quantity

Rating

Exceptional		Smokable	
Most Enjoyable		Poor	

Affix Cigar Band Here

Tasting Notes

Appearance/Ash
Burn/Draw
Flavor/Strength
Overall Impressions

Tasting Experience

> *A good Cuban cigar closes the door to the vulgarities of the world.*
>
> ❦
>
> Franz Liszt

Date Tasted

Place

Occasion

Tasting Companion(s)

Accompanying Libations

Overall Memories

Cigar Notes

Brand	
Region/Country	
Vintage	
Length	
Ring Gauge	
Date Purchased	
Place of Purchase	
Price/Quantity	

Rating

Exceptional	Smokable
Most Enjoyable	Poor

Affix Cigar Band Here

Tasting Notes

Appearance/Ash
Burn/Draw
Flavor/Strength
Overall Impressions

Tasting Experience

Date Tasted

Place

Occasion

Tasting Companion(s)

Accompanying Libations

Overall Memories

Cigar Notes

Brand
Region/Country
Vintage
Length
Ring Gauge
Date Purchased
Place of Purchase
Price/Quantity

Rating

Exceptional		Smokable
Most Enjoyable		Poor

Affix Cigar Band Here

Tasting Notes

Appearance/Ash
Burn/Draw
Flavor/Strength
Overall Impressions

Tasting Experience

Date Tasted	
Place	
Occasion	
Tasting Companion(s)	
Accompanying Libations	
Overall Memories	

Cigar Notes

Brand
Region/Country
Vintage
Length
Ring Gauge
Date Purchased
Place of Purchase
Price/Quantity

Rating

Exceptional		Smokable	
Most Enjoyable		Poor	

Affix Cigar Band Here

Tasting Notes

Appearance/Ash
Burn/Draw
Flavor/Strength
Overall Impressions

Tasting Experience

A well-chosen cigar is like armor and is useful against the torments of life.

Zino Davidoff

Date Tasted

Place

Occasion

Tasting Companion(s)

Accompanying Libations

Overall Memories

Cigar Notes

Brand

Region/Country

Vintage

Length

Ring Gauge

Date Purchased

Place of Purchase

Price/Quantity

Rating

Exceptional

Most Enjoyable

Smokable

Poor

Affix Cigar Band Here

Tasting Notes

Appearance/Ash

Burn/Draw

Flavor/Strength

Overall Impressions

Tasting Experience

Date Tasted

Place

Occasion

Tasting Companion(s)

Accompanying Libations

Overall Memories

Cigar Notes

Brand

Region/Country

Vintage

Length

Ring Gauge

Date Purchased

Place of Purchase

Price/Quantity

Rating

Exceptional

Smokable

Most Enjoyable

Poor

Affix Cigar Band Here

Tasting Notes

Appearance/Ash

Burn/Draw

Flavor/Strength

Overall Impressions

Tasting Experience

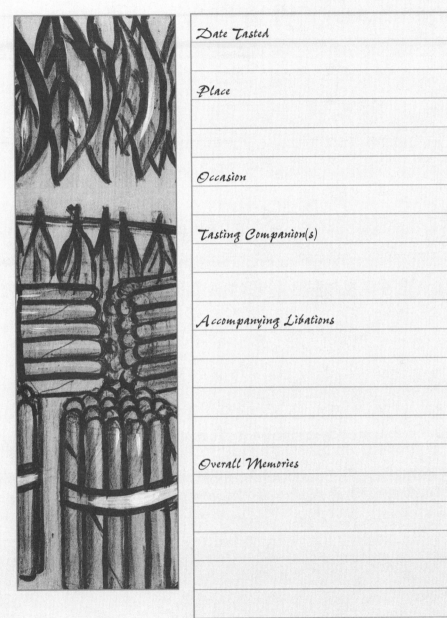

Date Tasted

Place

Occasion

Tasting Companion(s)

Accompanying Libations

Overall Memories

Cigar Notes

Brand
Region/Country
Vintage
Length
Ring Gauge
Date Purchased
Place of Purchase
Price/Quantity

Rating

Exceptional		Smokable	
Most Enjoyable		Poor	

Affix Cigar Band Here

Tasting Notes

Appearance/Ash
Burn/Draw
Flavor/Strength
Overall Impressions

Tasting Experience

Sometimes, madam,
a cigar is just a
cigar.

— ❦ —

Sigmund Freud

Date Tasted

Place

Occasion

Tasting Companion(s)

Accompanying Libations

Overall Memories

Cigar Notes

Brand
Region/Country
Vintage
Length
Ring Gauge
Date Purchased
Place of Purchase
Price/Quantity

Rating

Exceptional		Smokable	
Most Enjoyable		Poor	

Affix Cigar Band Here

Tasting Notes

Appearance/Ash
Burn/Draw
Flavor/Strength
Overall Impressions

Tasting Experience

Date Tasted

Place

Occasion

Tasting Companion(s)

Accompanying Libations

Overall Memories

Cigar Notes

Brand
Region/Country
Vintage
Length
Ring Gauge
Date Purchased
Place of Purchase
Price/Quantity

Rating

Exceptional	Smokable	
Most Enjoyable	Poor	

Affix Cigar Band Here

Tasting Notes

Appearance/Ash
Burn/Draw
Flavor/Strength
Overall Impressions

Tasting Experience

Date Tasted

Place

Occasion

Tasting Companion(s)

Accompanying Libations

Overall Memories

Cigar Notes

Brand
Region/Country
Vintage
Length
Ring Gauge
Date Purchased
Place of Purchase
Price/Quantity

Rating

Exceptional		Smokable	
Most Enjoyable		Poor	

Affix Cigar Band Here

Tasting Notes

Appearance/Ash
Burn/Draw
Flavor/Strength
Overall Impressions

Tasting Experience

Date Tasted

Place

Occasion

Tasting Companion(s)

Accompanying Libations

Overall Memories

Cigar Notes

Brand	
Region/Country	
Vintage	
Length	
Ring Gauge	
Date Purchased	
Place of Purchase	
Price/Quantity	

Rating

Exceptional		Smokable	
Most Enjoyable		Poor	

Affix Cigar Band Here

Tasting Notes

Appearance/Ash
Burn/Draw
Flavor/Strength
Overall Impressions

Tasting Experience

Date Tasted	
Place	
Occasion	
Tasting Companion(s)	
Accompanying Libations	
Overall Memories	

Cigar Notes

Brand
Region/Country
Vintage
Length
Ring Gauge
Date Purchased
Place of Purchase
Price/Quantity

Rating

Exceptional		Smokable	
Most Enjoyable		Poor	

Affix Cigar Band Here

Tasting Notes

Appearance/Ash
Burn/Draw
Flavor/Strength
Overall Impressions

Tasting Experience

Date Tasted

Place

Occasion

Tasting Companion(s)

Accompanying Libations

Overall Memories

Cigar Notes

Brand
_____

_____

Region/Country
_____

_____

Vintage
_____

Length
_____

Ring Gauge
_____

Date Purchased
_____

Place of Purchase
_____

_____

Price/Quantity
_____

_____

Rating

Exceptional   Smokable

Most Enjoyable   Poor

Affix Cigar Brand Here

Tasting Notes

Appearance/Ash
_____

_____

Burn/Draw
_____

_____

Flavor/Strength
_____

_____

Overall Impressions
_____

_____

_____

Tasting Experience

> *I smoke in moderation. Only one cigar at a time.*
>
> ❖
>
> Samuel Clemens
> (a.k.a. Mark Twain)

Date Tasted

Place

Occasion

Tasting Companion(s)

Accompanying Libations

Overall Memories

Cigar Notes

Brand

Region/Country

Vintage

Length

Ring Gauge

Date Purchased

Place of Purchase

Price/Quantity

Rating

Exceptional

Most Enjoyable

Smokable

Poor

Affix Cigar Band Here

Tasting Notes

Appearance/Ash

Burn/Draw

Flavor/Strength

Overall Impressions

Tasting Experience

Date Tasted

Place

Occasion

Tasting Companion(s)

Accompanying Libations

Overall Memories

Cigar Notes

Brand
Region/Country
Vintage
Length
Ring Gauge
Date Purchased
Place of Purchase
Price/Quantity

Rating

Exceptional

Most Enjoyable

Smokable

Poor

Affix Cigar Band Here

Tasting Notes

Appearance/Ash

Burn/Draw

Flavor/Strength

Overall Impressions

Tasting Experience

Date Tasted

Place

Occasion

Tasting Companion(s)

Accompanying Libations

Overall Memories

Cigar Notes

Brand
Region/Country
Vintage
Length
Ring Gauge
Date Purchased
Place of Purchase
Price/Quantity

Rating

Exceptional

Most Enjoyable

Smokable

Poor

Affix Cigar Band Here

Tasting Notes

Appearance/Ash
Burn/Draw
Flavor/Strength
Overall Impressions

Tasting Experience

> I vow and believe
> that the cigar has
> been one of the
> greatest creature-
> comforts of my life —
> a kind companion, a
> gentle stimulant, an
> amiable anodyne, a
> cementer of
> friendship. May I die
> if I abuse that
> kindly weed which
> has given me so
> much pleasure!
>
> —◆—
>
> William Makepeace
> Thackeray

Date Tasted

Place

Occasion

Tasting Companion(s)

Accompanying Libations

Overall Memories

Cigar Notes

Brand
Region/Country
Vintage
Length
Ring Gauge
Date Purchased
Place of Purchase
Price/Quantity

Rating

Exceptional		Smokable	
Most Enjoyable		Poor	

Affix Cigar Band Here

Tasting Notes

Appearance/Ash

Burn/Draw

Flavor/Strength

Overall Impressions

Tasting Experience

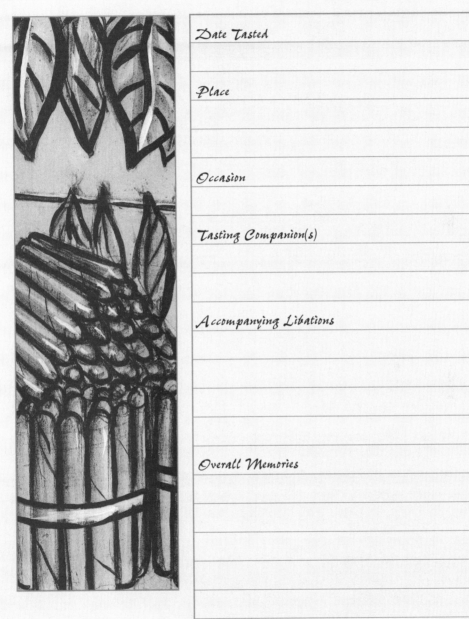

Date Tasted

Place

Occasion

Tasting Companion(s)

Accompanying Libations

Overall Memories

Cigar Notes

Brand
Region/Country
Vintage
Length
Ring Gauge
Date Purchased
Place of Purchase
Price/Quantity

Rating

Exceptional

Most Enjoyable

Smokable

Poor

Affix Cigar Band Here

Tasting Notes

Appearance/Ash
Burn/Draw
Flavor/Strength
Overall Impressions

Tasting Experience

Date Tasted

Place

Occasion

Tasting Companion(s)

Accompanying Libations

Overall Memories

Cigar Notes

Brand	
Region/Country	
Vintage	
Length	
Ring Gauge	
Date Purchased	
Place of Purchase	
Price/Quantity	

Rating

Exceptional		Smokable	
Most Enjoyable		Poor	

Affix Cigar Band Here

Tasting Notes

Appearance/Ash	
Burn/Draw	
Flavor/Strength	
Overall Impressions	

Tasting Experience

A cigar numbs sorrow and fills the solitary hours with a million gracious images.

George Sand

Date Tasted

Place

Occasion

Tasting Companion(s)

Accompanying Libations

Overall Memories

Cigar Notes

Brand	
Region/Country	
Vintage	
Length	
Ring Gauge	
Date Purchased	
Place of Purchase	
Price/Quantity	

Rating

Exceptional		Smokable	
Most Enjoyable		Poor	

Affix Cigar Band Here

Tasting Notes

Appearance/Ash
Burn/Draw
Flavor/Strength
Overall Impressions

Tasting Experience

Date Tasted

Place

Occasion

Tasting Companion(s)

Accompanying Libations

Overall Memories

Cigar Notes

Brand
Region/Country
Vintage
Length
Ring Gauge
Date Purchased
Place of Purchase
Price/Quantity

Rating

Exceptional

Smokable

Most Enjoyable

Poor

Affix Cigar Band Here

Tasting Notes

Appearance/Ash
Burn/Draw
Flavor/Strength
Overall Impressions

Tasting Experience

Date Tasted

Place

Occasion

Tasting Companion(s)

Accompanying Libations

Overall Memories

Cigar Notes

Brand
Region/Country
Vintage
Length
Ring Gauge
Date Purchased
Place of Purchase
Price/Quantity

Rating

Exceptional

Most Enjoyable

Smokable

Poor

Affix Cigar Band Here

Tasting Notes

Appearance/Ash
Burn/Draw
Flavor/Strength
Overall Impressions

Tasting Experience

*… I promised
myself that if ever I
had some money
that I would savor a
cigar each day after
lunch and dinner.
This is the only
resolution of my
youth that I have
kept, and the only
realized ambition
which has not
brought disillusion.*

Somerset Maugham

Date Tasted

Place

Occasion

Tasting Companion(s)

Accompanying Libations

Overall Memories

Cigar Notes

Brand
Region/Country
Vintage
Length
Ring Gauge
Date Purchased
Place of Purchase
Price/Quantity

Rating

Exceptional		Smokable	
Most Enjoyable		Poor	

Affix Cigar Band Here

Tasting Notes

Appearance/Ash
Burn/Draw
Flavor/Strength
Overall Impressions

Tasting Experience

Date Tasted

Place

Occasion

Tasting Companion(s)

Accompanying Libations

Overall Memories

Cigar Notes

Brand
Region/Country
Vintage
Length
Ring Gauge
Date Purchased
Place of Purchase
Price/Quantity

Rating

Exceptional		Smokable	
Most Enjoyable		Poor	

Affix Cigar Band Here

Tasting Notes

Appearance/Ash
Burn/Draw
Flavor/Strength
Overall Impressions

Tasting Experience

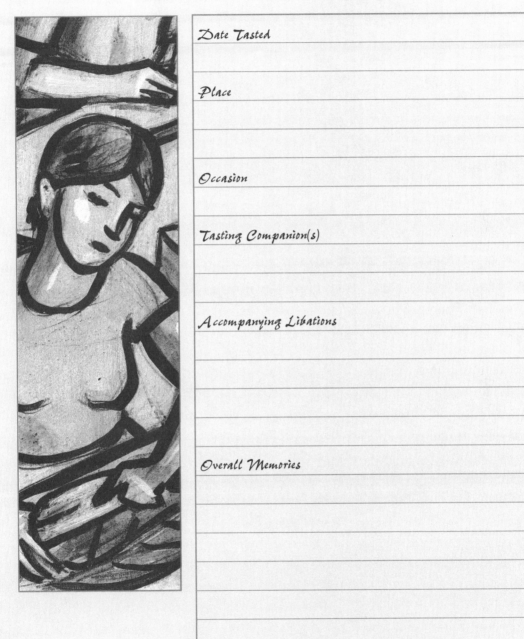

Date Tasted

Place

Occasion

Tasting Companion(s)

Accompanying Libations

Overall Memories

Cigar Notes

Brand
Region/Country
Vintage
Length
Ring Gauge
Date Purchased
Place of Purchase
Price/Quantity

Rating

Exceptional

Most Enjoyable

Smokable

Poor

Affix Cigar Band Here

Tasting Notes

Appearance/Ash
Burn/Draw
Flavor/Strength
Overall Impressions

Tasting Experience

Love is like a cigar.
If it goes out, you
can light it again,
but it never tastes
quite the same.

Archibald Percival

Wavell

Date Tasted

Place

Occasion

Tasting Companion(s)

Accompanying Libations

Overall Memories

Cigar Notes

Brand	
Region/Country	
Vintage	
Length	
Ring Gauge	
Date Purchased	
Place of Purchase	
Price/Quantity	

Rating

Exceptional		Smokable	
Most Enjoyable		Poor	

Affix Cigar Band Here

Tasting Notes

Appearance/Ash
Burn/Draw
Flavor/Strength
Overall Impressions

Tasting Experience

Date Tasted

Place

Occasion

Tasting Companion(s)

Accompanying Libations

Overall Memories

Cigar Notes

Brand
Region/Country
Vintage
Length
Ring Gauge
Date Purchased
Place of Purchase
Price/Quantity

Rating

Exceptional

Most Enjoyable

Smokable

Poor

Affix Cigar Band Here

Tasting Notes

Appearance/Ash
Burn/Draw
Flavor/Strength
Overall Impressions

Tasting Experience

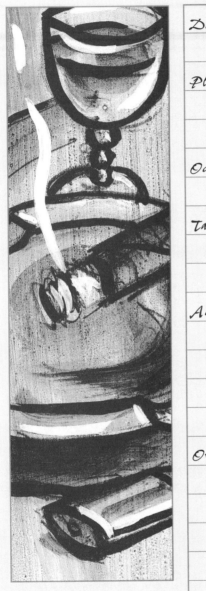

Date Tasted

Place

Occasion

Tasting Companion(s)

Accompanying Libations

Overall Memories

Cigar Notes

Brand	
Region/Country	
Vintage	
Length	
Ring Gauge	
Date Purchased	
Place of Purchase	
Price/Quantity	

Rating

Exceptional

Smokable

Most Enjoyable

Poor

Affix Cigar Band Here

Tasting Notes

Appearance/Ash
Burn/Draw
Flavor/Strength
Overall Impressions

Tasting Experience

… my spirit is led into the enchanted palaces of imagination – carried by the pale blue clouds of a fragrant Havana …

Alexander VerHuell

Date Tasted

Place

Occasion

Tasting Companion(s)

Accompanying Libations

Overall Memories

Cigar Notes

Brand
Region/Country
Vintage
Length
Ring Gauge
Date Purchased
Place of Purchase
Price/Quantity

Rating

Exceptional		Smokable	
Most Enjoyable		Poor	

Affix Cigar Band Here

Tasting Notes

Appearance/Ash
Burn/Draw
Flavor/Strength
Overall Impressions

Tasting Experience

Date Tasted
Place
Occasion
Tasting Companion(s)
Accompanying Libations
Overall Memories

Cigar Notes

Brand	
Region/Country	
Vintage	
Length	
Ring Gauge	
Date Purchased	
Place of Purchase	
Price/Quantity	

Rating

Exceptional		Smokable	
Most Enjoyable		Poor	

Affix Cigar Band Here

Tasting Notes

Appearance/Ash
Burn/Draw
Flavor/Strength
Overall Impressions

Tasting Experience

Date Tasted

Place

Occasion

Tasting Companion(s)

Accompanying Libations

Overall Memories

Cigar Notes

Brand	
Region/Country	
Vintage	
Length	
Ring Gauge	
Date Purchased	
Place of Purchase	
Price/Quantity	

Rating

Exceptional

Most Enjoyable

Smokable

Poor

Affix Cigar Band Here

Tasting Notes

Appearance/Ash	
Burn/Draw	
Flavor/Strength	
Overall Impressions	

Tasting Experience

I always hold Cuba in my mouth.

❖

Winston Churchill

Date Tasted

Place

Occasion

Tasting Companion(s)

Accompanying Libations

Overall Memories

Cigar Notes

Brand
Region/Country
Vintage
Length
Ring Gauge
Date Purchased
Place of Purchase
Price/Quantity

Rating

Exceptional		Smokable	
Most Enjoyable		Poor	

Affix Cigar Band Here

Tasting Notes

Appearance/Ash
Burn/Draw
Flavor/Strength
Overall Impressions

Tasting Experience

Date Tasted
Place
Occasion
Tasting Companion(s)
Accompanying Libations
Overall Memories

Cigar Notes

Brand	
Region/Country	
Vintage	
Length	
Ring Gauge	
Date Purchased	
Place of Purchase	
Price/Quantity	

Rating

Exceptional		Smokable	
Most Enjoyable		Poor	

Affix Cigar Band Here

Tasting Notes

Appearance/Ash

Burn/Draw

Flavor/Strength

Overall Impressions

Tasting Experience

Date Tasted

Place

Occasion

Tasting Companion(s)

Accompanying Libations

Overall Memories

Cigar Notes

Brand	
Region/Country	
Vintage	
Length	
Ring Gauge	
Date Purchased	
Place of Purchase	
Price/Quantity	

Rating

Exceptional	Smokable	
Most Enjoyable	Poor	

Affix Cigar Band Here

Tasting Notes

Appearance/Ash
Burn/Draw
Flavor/Strength
Overall Impressions

Tasting Experience

I am done – pay the bills and get me a cigar.

———❦———

William Makepeace
Thackeray

Date Tasted

Place

Occasion

Tasting Companion(s)

Accompanying Libations

Overall Memories

Cigar Notes

Brand

Region/Country

Vintage

Length

Ring Gauge

Date Purchased

Place of Purchase

Price/Quantity

Rating

Exceptional

Smokable

Most Enjoyable

Poor

Affix Cigar Band Here

Tasting Notes

Appearance/Ash

Burn/Draw

Flavor/Strength

Overall Impressions

Tasting Experience

Date Tasted	
Place	
Occasion	
Tasting Companion(s)	
Accompanying Libations	
Overall Memories	

Cigar Notes

Brand
Region/Country
Vintage
Length
Ring Gauge
Date Purchased
Place of Purchase
Price/Quantity

Rating

Exceptional		Smokable	
Most Enjoyable		Poor	

Affix Cigar Band Here

Tasting Notes

Appearance/Ash
Burn/Draw
Flavor/Strength
Overall Impressions

Tasting Experience

Date Tasted

Place

Occasion

Tasting Companion(s)

Accompanying Libations

Overall Memories

Cigar Notes

Brand
Region/Country
Vintage
Length
Ring Gauge
Date Purchased
Place of Purchase
Price/Quantity

Rating

Exceptional		Smokable	
Most Enjoyable		Poor	

Affix Cigar Band Here

Tasting Notes

Appearance/Ash
Burn/Draw
Flavor/Strength
Overall Impressions

Tasting Experience

The cigar is a great resource…. Are you subject to aches and pains (or bad temper)? The cigar will change your disposition. Are you harassed by unpleasant thoughts? Smoking a cigar puts one in a frame of mind to dispense with these….

Duc de la Rochefoucauld–Liancourt

Date Tasted

Place

Occasion

Tasting Companion(s)

Accompanying Libations

Overall Memories

Cigar Notes

Brand

_____

Region/Country

_____

Vintage

_____

Length

_____

Ring Gauge

_____

Date Purchased

_____

Place of Purchase

_____

Price/Quantity

_____

Rating

Exceptional

Most Enjoyable

Smokable

Poor

Affix Cigar Band Here

Tasting Notes

Appearance/Ash

_____

Burn/Draw

_____

Flavor/Strength

_____

Overall Impressions

_____

Tasting Experience

Date Tasted

Place

Occasion

Tasting Companion(s)

Accompanying Libations

Overall Memories

Cigar Notes

Brand
Region/Country
Vintage
Length
Ring Gauge
Date Purchased
Place of Purchase
Price/Quantity

Rating

Exceptional		Smokable	
Most Enjoyable		Poor	

Affix Cigar Band Here

Tasting Notes

Appearance/Ash
Burn/Draw
Flavor/Strength
Overall Impressions

Tasting Experience

Date Tasted

Place

Occasion

Tasting Companion(s)

Accompanying Libations

Overall Memories

Cigar Notes

Brand
Region/Country
Vintage
Length
Ring Gauge
Date Purchased
Place of Purchase
Price/Quantity

Rating

Exceptional

Smokable

Most Enjoyable

Poor

Affix Cigar Band Here

Tasting Notes

Appearance/Ash
Burn/Draw
Flavor/Strength
Overall Impressions

The cigar exhibits "the eternal attributes of prestige, success and savoir faire."

━━◆◆◆━━

Italo Calvino

Date Tasted	
Place	
Occasion	
Tasting Companion(s)	
Accompanying Libations	
Overall Memories	

Cigars to Try Next Time

Cigars to Try Next Time

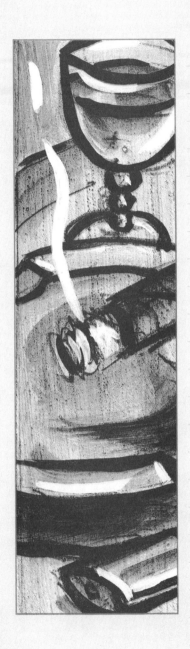

Cigars to Try Next Time

Cigars to Try Next Time

> *... the whole island of Cuba is a natural humidor.*
>
> Bernard Wolfe

Cigars to Try Next Time

Cigars to Try Next Time

Addresses & Contact Numbers

Name	Name
Address	Address
Phone	Phone
Fax	Fax
E-mail	E-mail
Name	Name
Address	Address
Phone	Phone
Fax	Fax
E-mail	E-mail
Name	Name
Address	Address
Phone	Phone
Fax	Fax
E-mail	E-mail

Addresses & Contact Numbers

Name	Name
Address	Address
Phone	Phone
Fax	Fax
E-mail	E-mail
Name	Name
Address	Address
Phone	Phone
Fax	Fax
E-mail	E-mail
Name	Name
Address	Address
Phone	Phone
Fax	Fax
E-mail	E-mail

Addresses & Contact Numbers

Name	Name
Address	Address
Phone	Phone
Fax	Fax
E-mail	E-mail
Name	Name
Address	Address
Phone	Phone
Fax	Fax
E-mail	E-mail
Name	Name
Address	Address
Phone	Phone
Fax	Fax
E-mail	E-mail

Addresses & Contact Numbers

Name	Name
Address	Address
Phone	Phone
Fax	Fax
E-mail	E-mail
Name	Name
Address	Address
Phone	Phone
Fax	Fax
E-mail	E-mail
Name	Name
Address	Address
Phone	Phone
Fax	Fax
E-mail	E-mail

Addresses & Contact Numbers

Name	Name
Address	Address
Phone	Phone
Fax	Fax
E-mail	E-mail
Name	Name
Address	Address
Phone	Phone
Fax	Fax
E-mail	E-mail
Name	Name
Address	Address
Phone	Phone
Fax	Fax
E-mail	E-mail

Addresses & Contact Numbers

Name	Name
Address	Address
Phone	Phone
Fax	Fax
E-mail	E-mail
Name	Name
Address	Address
Phone	Phone
Fax	Fax
E-mail	E-mail
Name	Name
Address	Address
Phone	Phone
Fax	Fax
E-mail	E-mail

Cigar Labels & Miscellanea

Cigar Labels & Miscellanea

Cigar Labels & Miscellanea

Cigar Labels & Miscellanea

Cigar Labels & Miscellanea

Cigar Labels & Miscellanea

Cigar Labels & Miscellanea

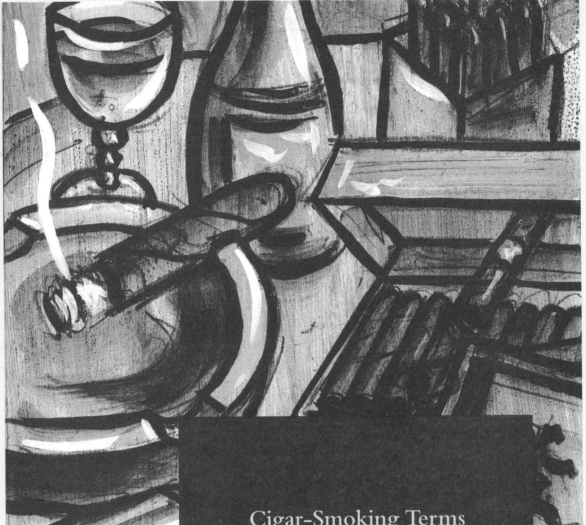

Cigar-Smoking Terms

Cigar-Smoking Terms

Just as the cigar's flavors have evolved and increased over time, so too has the body of words associated with cigar-smoking. To help you fill in the pages of this journal (or to talk the talk of a true connoisseur), here is a list of some of the most common terms used in the language of cigars.

Ash

Evaluation of the color and structure of a cigar's ash is an important part of the cigar-tasting process. The whiter the ash, the better the soil in which the tobacco was grown, and a long, evenly formed ash is a sign of a well-constructed cigar.

Binder

The tobacco leaf that holds the filler of the cigar together. Chosen for its durability, the binder is normally a coarse leaf that is often found on the upper part of the tobacco plant.

Blend

The mixture of different tobacco leaves that make up a cigar. It is the blend of filler leaves that gives the cigar its flavor and strength.

Boîte Nature

The cedar box in which many cigars are sold. Packing cigars in cedar boxes dates back to 1830, when the bank of H. Upmann sent its directors cigars in boxes much like the ones we are familiar with today. The bank eventually went into the cigar business, and the cedar box soon caught on with other cigar manufacturers.

Cigar-Smoking Terms

Bouquet
The aroma (or "nose") of a cigar. Simply put, a high-quality cigar will smell more fragrant than an inferior one, both before it is lit and while it is burning.

Cap
A small, round piece of wrapper leaf attached to the head of a cigar. The purpose of the cap is to secure the wrapper.

Cigar Band
The ring of paper that sits near the head of a cigar. The invention of the cigar band is attributed to a Dutch cigar manufacturer named Gustave Bock, who in 1850 developed this means of labeling his cigars in order to distinguish them from other brands. Today cigar bands often indicate the brand name and country of origin of the product as well as whether or not it was hand-rolled.

Draw
The rate at which air is pulled through a lit cigar. A cigar's draw should be smooth and easy. If it draws quickly and fills your mouth with hot rather than cool, tasty smoke, it is a poorly made cigar. Similarly, if the cigar is hard to draw on, or if it goes out two or three times before you've smoked a third of it, it has likely been wrapped too tightly.

Filler
The tobacco leaves that make up the body of a cigar. A combination of leaves from the top, middle and bottom of the tobacco plant are normally used for the filler.

Cigar-Smoking Terms

Foot

The end of the cigar that you light. The foot of a cigar is usually pre-cut.

Head

The closed end of a cigar. The head of a handmade cigar must be clipped or cut about 1/8th of an inch (3 millimeters) before the foot is lit.

Hot

A term used to describe a cigar that has a quick draw.

Humidor

A hermetically sealed box used to preserve and properly age cigars. Humidors are constructed of various types of woods, but their interiors should always be lined with Spanish cedar (its natural oils prevent the cigars from drying out). Humidors can range in price from $200 to $5,000.

Plugged

A term used to describe a cigar that has a difficult draw.

Ring Gauge

The thickness, or diameter, of a cigar, measured in 1/64ths of an inch (or 0.4 millimeters). A cigar with a ring gauge of 32, for example, is 32/64ths of an inch (or 12.5 millimeters) in diameter.

Cigar-Smoking Terms

Stogie

An informal term for *cigar*, it is sometimes used to describe a smoke of inferior quality. The term *stogie* derives from the word Conestoga, a town in Pennsylvania where a special cigar was produced and subsequently became popular with the teamsters who drove the famed Conestoga wagons westward across America.

Tunneling

The unpleasant occurrence of a cigar burning unevenly. To prevent tunneling, rotate your cigar occasionally while you are smoking it.

Vintage

Sometimes used to identify a cigar, vintage refers to the year the tobacco was harvested and *not* the year the cigar was made.

Vistas

The colorful images that adorn the tops of cigar boxes. Today vintage vistas are avidly collected and can often fetch thousands of dollars.

Wrapper

The high-quality tobacco leaf that is wrapped around the filler and binder of a cigar. A cigar's wrapper should be perfect: no wrinkles, spots, veins or tears should be evident.

Notes

Notes

ALSO AVAILABLE FROM RAINCOAST BOOKS

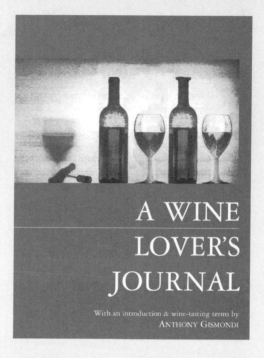